Unit 1

Word Bank

 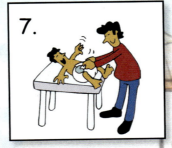 

arrive sell travel
skate whistle visit
follow swing change
leave study answer

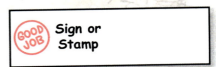

Sign or Stamp

Practice together as a class and then see if you can do it by yourself! Have lots of activities to practice making past tense sentences with these verbs.

Verb	Past Tense	Verb	Past Tense
talk	talked	fall	fell
buy	bought	draw	drew
jump	jumped	give	gave
read	read	hide	hid
open	opened	throw	threw
follow	followed	play	played
look	looked	say	said
skate	skated	ride	rode
take	took	write	wrote
see	saw	leave	left
be	was/were	have	had
make	made	sleep	slept
arrive	arrived	listen	listened
eat	ate	hear	heard
watch	watched	catch	caught
go	went	fly	flew
run	ran	sing	sang
fight	fought	break	broke

Scripted Sentence Starters

	+	?	−	🕐
Present Tense:	verb (He/She/It) -> S	Do/Does	(don't/doesn't)	every day
Present Cont:	be verb + verb + ing	Be-Verb	(am not/isn't/aren't)	right now
Future Tense:	be verb + going to + verb	Be-Verb	(am not/isn't/aren't)	tomorrow
Past Tense:	verb + ed (ate, hid, fell)	Did	didn't	yesterday

1. he  every day
2.  right now
3.  tomorrow
4. yesterday

5. the girls  every day
6.  right now
7.  this weekend
8.  last weekend

You can change underlined words (or any other words).

1. What does he do every day? He <u>rides a bike</u>.
2. What is he doing right now? He is <u>riding a bike</u>.
3. What is he going to do tomorrow? He is going to <u>ride a bike</u>.
4. What did he do yesterday? He <u>rode his bike</u>.

Record Audio or Speak With the Teacher

4 = bronze
6 = silver
8 = gold

 Sign or Stamp

3

My Favorite Activities

My name is Yu Yan. I have many interests, but here are my top three.

First, I like to learn new things. I think school is the coolest place ever. I have some really great teachers and they are always telling me about things I didn't know. When I go home, I tell my parents about the things I learned,is and they ask lots of questions.

Skating is another one of my favorite activities. I go to the ice skating rink once a week to skate. I have my own skates that my parents bought me. I like to skate around the ice really fast. I am learning how to skate backwards, but I fall down a lot.

Finally, I love to talk. Whenever I see my friends, we talk about all kinds of things. We talk about class. We talk about our favorite TV shows. We talk about the mean fifth grader we always hide from. When I am with my friends, we talk in Chinese. I can't talk very well in English yet, but I am getting better.

I love to learn, skate and talk. I have lots more interests as well, but these are my top three. What are your top three interests?

Record Audio or Read to the Teacher

Sign or Stamp

Unit 2

Word Bank

 1.
 2.
 3.
 4.
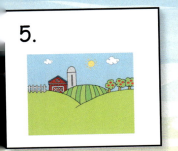 5.
 6.
 7.
 8.
 9.
 10.
 11.
 12.

dentist office
bookstore
movie theater
bus stop

library
museum
ocean
pet store

beach
farm
castle
forest

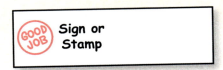 Sign or Stamp

Practice together as a class and then see if you can do it by yourself! Play lots of games to practice making past tense sentences with these verbs.

Verb	Past Tense	Verb	Past Tense
talk		fall	
buy		draw	
jump		give	
read		hide	
open		throw	
follow		play	
look		say	
skate		ride	
take		write	
see		leave	
be		have	
make		sleep	
arrive		listen	
eat		hear	
watch		catch	
go		fly	
run		sing	
fight		break	

Sentence Starter Conversation

1. Where does your friend go every day? What does he/she do there?
2. Where is he/she right now? What is he/she doing there?
3. Where is he/she going to go tomorrow? What is he/she going to do there?
4. Where did he/she go yesterday? What did he/she do there?

You can change underlined words (or any other words).

1. He goes to <u>the library</u> every day. He <u>reads books</u>.
2. He is at the <u>dentist</u> right now. He is <u>getting his teeth cleaned</u>.
3. He is going to go to <u>the beach</u> tomorrow. He is going to <u>swim</u>.
4. He went to <u>a park</u> yesterday. He <u>rode his bicycle</u>.

Record Audio or Speak With the Teacher

4 = bronze
6 = silver
8 = gold

 Sign or Stamp

7

Museums and Libraries

Museums and libraries are important places. They are similar in some ways and different in others. Let's take a closer look.

Libraries and museums are similar in that they both give people the chance to learn new things. When you go to a library, you can learn new things through books. When you go to a museum, you can learn new things through the exhibits. If you want to learn about dinosaurs, for instance, you can find information about them in books at the library or at exhibits in a natural history museum.

Libraries and museums are different as well. Libraries have books on any topic you might be interested in. Museums generally focus on one theme, like history, or science, for instance. Libraries also carry fiction, books with stories that are not real. Museums focus on facts, things that are true, not fiction.

Libraries and museums are both similar and different, but they are both important places.

Record Audio or Read to the Teacher

Unit 3

Word Bank

1.
2.
3.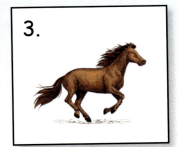
4.
5.
6.
7.
8.
9.
10.
11.
12.

queen
cowboy
detective
pirate

dolphin
clue
horse
Native American
(Indian)

poison
whale
mirror
treasure

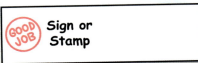
Sign or Stamp

Practice together as a class and then see if you can do it by yourself! Play lots of games to practice making past tense sentences with these verbs.

Verb	Past Tense	Verb	Past Tense
talk		fall	
buy		draw	
jump		give	
read		hide	
open		throw	
follow		play	
look		say	
skate		ride	
take		write	
see		leave	
be		have	
make		sleep	
arrive		listen	
eat		hear	
watch		catch	
go		fly	
run		sing	
fight		break	

Be-Verb Questions and Answers

1. You/I
2. He
3. They

Count/Non-count Nouns

4.
5.
6.
7.

This, That, These, Those

8.
9.
10.
11.

1. Are you hungry? Yes, I am.
2. Is he a thief? Yes, he is.
3. Are they sick? Yes, they are.
4. How much homework do you have?
   I have a lot of homework.
5. How many guitars are there?
   There are two guitars.
6. How much money is there?
   There is a lot of money.
7. How many clues are there?
   There are a lot of clues.
8. Is this a hippo? Yes, it is.
9. Is that a lion? Yes, it is.
10. Are these cats? No, they aren't.
11. Are those birds? No, they aren't.

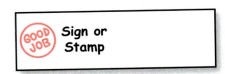

STORIES

The world is full of great stories. But did you know that just about every story follows the same structure?

First, there is a beginning to every story. This is where the characters and the setting are introduced. For instance, you meet a princess, a pirate, a detective, or a cowboy. Those are the characters. Then, the setting is introduced. The princess lives in a castle a long, long time ago. The pirate wakes up in the morning on his pirate ship. The detective is sitting in his office when an old lady comes in the door. The cowboy is riding his horse under a hot afternoon sun.

Then, what happens next? You guessed it. There is a problem. A mean old queen gives the princess some poison. The pirate falls into shark-infested waters when he is looking for treasure. The detective needs to find the thief who stole the old lady's car. The cowboy's horse gets scared by a snake, throws the cowboy on the ground, and runs away. What are they going to do? How are they going to solve the problem?

Usually, someone helps the character. A prince kisses the princess and she gets better. Some dolphins save the pirate and the pirate decides to start a new life helping whales and dolphins. The old lady's neighbor tells the detective that no one stole the car; The old lady parked it at the wrong house. A Native American finds the horse and returns it to the cowboy. The cowboy cries tears of joy and gives the Native American a big hug.

In the end, everything usually turns out alright. There is a happy ending. That is how almost every story goes. Can you think of a story and name the characters, setting, problem, and solution?

Unit 4

Word Bank

1.
2.
3.
4.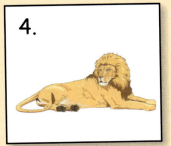
5.
6.
7.
8.
9.
10.
11.
12.

stare
spill
quiet
silent

lazy
patient
careless
lie down

pounce
approach
examine
criminal

 Sign or Stamp

Adjectives

He is loud.
The loud boy is yelling in the classroom.

1.
2.
3.
4.
5.
6.
7.
8.

Record Audio or Speak With the Teacher
 4 = bronze
6 = silver
8 = gold

 Sign or Stamp

1. The <u>angry</u> teacher <u>stares at me</u> every day.
2. The <u>careless</u> lady <u>spilled the coffee</u>.
3. The <u>happy</u> man is going to <u>dive in the water</u>.
4. The <u>silent</u> boy <u>hid in the trash can</u> last night.
5. The <u>patient</u> man <u>waits for the elevator</u> every morning.
6. The <u>lazy</u> lion is <u>lying down on the ground</u>.
7. The <u>careful</u> woman is going to <u>examine the money</u> this afternoon
8. The <u>silent</u> criminal <u>approached the bank</u> last night.

Story Challenge

Goal: To be able to say and write out the story by memory with fewer than 3 mistakes.

1. Read through and act out as a class.
2. As a class, cover the paragraph, say it and act it out.
3. Get with a partner and practice memorizing it together.
4. Be able to say it by memory with fewer than 3 mistakes.
5. Be able to write it out by memory with fewer than 3 mistakes.
6. Change it to make it your own.

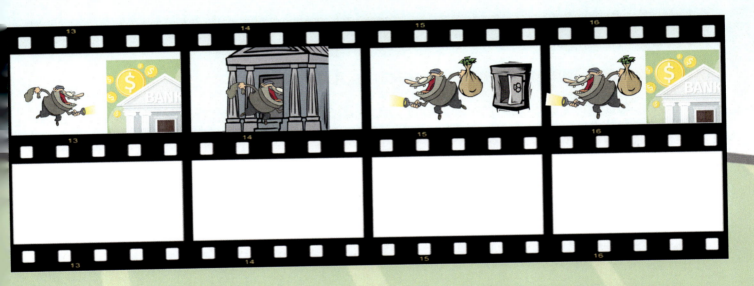

A patient criminal approached an old bank one night and broke in. He was very quiet. He stole a lot of money. Then he left. When he got home, he was excited.

But then he examined the money. It was fake money!

"Don't move!" came a voice from outside.

Police broke down his door and pounced on him. Now the careless criminal is lying in jail.

 Sign or Stamp

THE SCARY LION and the CUTE BUNNIES

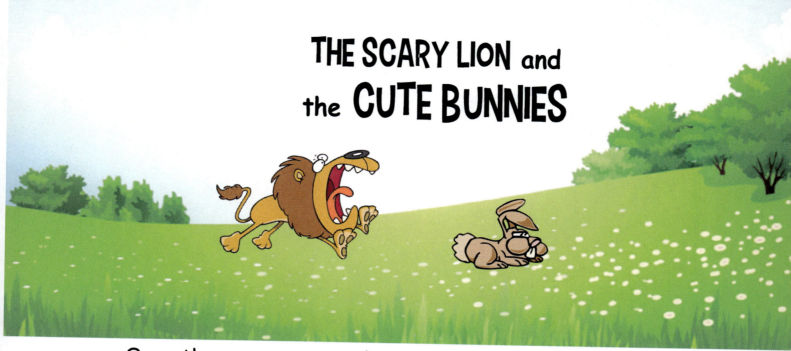

Once there was a scary lion. It liked to eat anything and everything. It ate twenty animals a day. It caught hippos for breakfast and elephants for dinner. It was so frightening that if it was sleeping, and an animal approached it, the animal died.

One day, the scary lion was walking through a forest when it saw a cute little rabbit. The lion was patient. It lay down and waited for a few minutes. Then it quietly approached the rabbit. The rabbit looked delicious.

When the lion was really close, it pounced. It opened its big, scary mouth to eat the rabbit, but, right when it was about to eat the rabbit, the rabbit moved, and the lion fell on its nose.

The cute little rabbit whistled for all of his little rabbit buddies. The rabbits all pounced on the lion and tickled it mercilessly.

"That will teach you to go around eating and scaring everything!" shouted the cute little rabbits.

The lion was so frightened that it ran away and only ever ate vegetables for the rest of its life.

Discussion Challenge

1. What three adjectives would you use to describe yourself?
2. Why is the biggest problem with being lazy?
3. When is the last time you were really careless?

Three adjectives I would use to describe myself would be _____ because _____.

The biggest problem with being lazy is _____ because _____. In order to _____, you need to _____.

The last time I was careless was _____. It happened like this. First... Then.... Suddenly... In the end...

- I agree with you about _____ because _____.

- I disagree with you about _____ because _____.

- I don't understand _____.
- Can you tell me more about _____.

- You're saying _____. Is that right?
- I like what you said about _____. I also think _____.

Sign or Stamp

Unit 5

Word Bank

1.

2.

3.

4.

5.

6.

7.

8.

9.

10.

11.

12.

show
explain
peek
musician

assistant
pilot
janitor
scientist

make-up artist
filmmaker
detective
programmer

Past Continuous Tense

Rules students should know about the past continuous tense.

Past Continuous: **was/were + verb + ing** (+)   **Was/Were** (?)   **wasn't/weren't** (−)   yesterday at 2:00
Be-verb = is, am, are, was, were

Structure of a Past Continuous Sentence

	Noun	Verb	Everything Else	When
1.	I	was jumping	on the bed	yesterday at 2:00
2.	You	were playing	at school	yesterday at 4:00
3.	They	were following	their mommy	yesterday at 6:00
4.	He	was eating	a hamburger	yesterday at 8:00
5.	She	was going	home	yesterday evening
6.	The dog	was sleeping	in a box	yesterday morning
7.	The dogs	were running		yesterday afternoon

Practice making gerunds out of the verbs below.

Verb + ing is usually pretty easy but sometimes...

Short Vowels: Double letter

1. cut -> _____
2. put -> _____
3. sit -> _____
4. dig -> _____
5. hug -> _____
6. shop -> _____

Ends in e:

7. take -> _____
8. bake -> _____
9. race -> _____
10. come -> _____
11. dance -> _____
12. hike -> _____

Scripted Sentence Starters

1.
2.
3.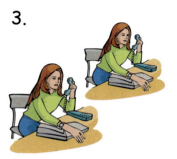
4.
5.
6.
7.
8.

Record Audio or Speak With the Teacher
4 = bronze
6 = silver
8 = gold

Sign or Stamp

1. What was the janitor doing yesterday at 2 PM? He was <u>cleaning the floors.</u>
2. What was the make-up artist doing yesterday at 9 AM? He was <u>putting on makeup</u>.
3. What were the assistants doing yesterday at noon? They were <u>answering the phone.</u>
4. What was the filmmaker doing yesterday at 3 PM? He was <u>filming a movie.</u>
5. What were the detectives doing last night? They were <u>looking for clues.</u>
6. What were the scientists doing yesterday morning? They were <u>doing experiments.</u>

How to Make Your Own Stop-Motion Movie

Did you know that with a cell phone, some Legos, and a little patience, you can be a filmmaker? You can. I'm going to tell you how.

First, you need a story to tell. You can write your own or retell a story someone else wrote. When you tell your story, you need to introduce your characters and setting. Afterward, a problem is going to happen and your characters need to find a solution to the problem.

Second, you need to build your scene and characters. This is where the Legos come in. Be sure to make the scenes look nice. Once you start filming, you won't be able to change them.

Next, you will need to set up your cell phone. You can use your phone's camera, but there is an even better way. You just need to search for a stop-motion app. There are many to choose from. These will let you take all your pictures, record your audio, add effects and title screens and lots more. Once you have the app you want to use ready to go, you will need to put your camera on a camera stand. You can set your phone on some books if you don't have a camera stand. You may also need a lamp next to your set.

Now that your scenes and your camera are set up, you are ready to film. Take your first picture. Make sure everything looks alright. Then start to move your first character into the scene. Take another picture. This is where the patience comes in. You need to take a lot of pictures. The more pictures you take of each little movement, the better the movie will be. Also, you will need to think about what your characters are doing during dialogue. While your characters talk, they can be moving their arms and turning their heads, for instance.

Now that you have taken all of those photos, record your audio and add a title screen. When you are finished, you can play it for your family and friends. Making your own stop-motion movie is a lot of fun.

Discussion Challenge

1. What do you want to be when you grow up?
2. What is the best job in the world? Why?
3. Explain what a janitor does and why this is an important job.

When I grow up, I want to be a _____. I want to be a _____ so that I can _____.

 • I agree with you about _____ because _____.

 • I disagree with you about _____ because _____.

I think the best job in the world is _____ because _____. Compared to other jobs, in this job, you can _____.

 • I don't understand _____.
• Can you tell me more about _____.

A janitor _____. Without janitors, _____. They deserve our respect and gratitude.

 • You're saying _____. Is that right?
• I like what you said about _____. I also think _____.

Rules:
- Speak 1 at a time.
- Respond to what others say by asking questions or making comments.

Sign or Stamp

Unit 6

Word Bank

1.
2.
3.
4.
5.
6.
7.
8.
9.
10.
11.

fix
grocery store
parents
flashlight

shiver
path
disappear
tiptoe

giggle
decide
map

 Sign or Stamp

Scripted Sentence Starters

1. My dad

2. The girl

3. you

4. Grandma

5. Edward

6. my teacher

Record Audio or Speak With the Teacher
 3 = bronze
4 = silver
6 = gold

 Sign or Stamp

You can change underlined words (or any other words).

1. My dad wasn't <u>fixing the car</u> yesterday at 9 PM.
2. The girl wasn't <u>explaining something to the doctor</u> this morning.
3. You weren't <u>giggling in class</u> this afternoon.
4. Grandma wasn't <u>shopping at the grocery store</u> on Sunday.
5. Edward wasn't <u>shivering</u> last night.
6. My teacher wasn't <u>tiptoeing past a lion</u> yesterday.

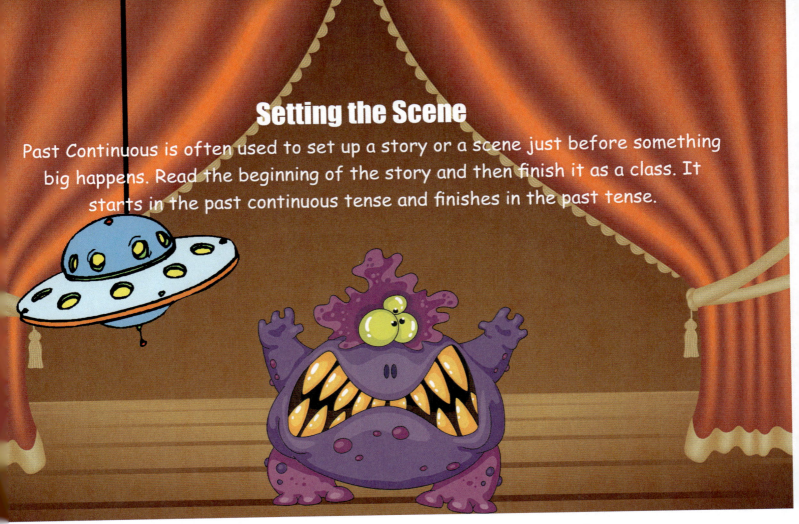

Setting the Scene

Past Continuous is often used to set up a story or a scene just before something big happens. Read the beginning of the story and then finish it as a class. It starts in the past continuous tense and finishes in the past tense.

Setting the Scene

There was a little theater on Main Street. They were putting on a show about aliens. Everyone was getting ready for the show. The janitor was cleaning. The camera operator was turning on the camera. An assistant was checking the set. Then, suddenly, a detective came into the theater.

"We need your help!" said the detective. "There are some real aliens outside, and they are angry about how they are being portrayed in your show!"

Ideas

Tie up

watch the show

chase

destroy

act

eat popcorn

Spotlight

One evening, not too long ago, it was getting late. My parents were busy. My dad was out fixing the car. My mom was at the grocery store. She was buying some groceries. I was playing with my brother in the backyard. We were playing Spotlight. It's like Hide and Seek with a flashlight.

I was looking for my brother, but couldn't find him anywhere. I was starting to get worried. My brother usually doesn't hide that well. Usually, he hides behind a tree with his feet sticking out and I find him in a few seconds. This time though, I was having trouble finding him. Behind our house, there is a large forest. A path leads into the forest from our yard.

"He wouldn't have gone down that path, right?" I said to myself. I looked down the path and shivered a little. I was kind of scared. I decided to tiptoe down the path a little. If there were any scary animals, I didn't want them to hear me.

"Boo!" my brother said loudly.

"Ahhh!" I screamed. My brother giggled.

"There you are! Where were you? I thought you had disappeared!" I yelled.

"I was hiding behind that tree," my brother replied.

"Wow! That's a good spot! I thought maybe a scary animal ate you," I said.

My brother laughed. "There's nothing in these woods," my brother said.

Then, suddenly, we heard a sound coming from the woods.

"Roar!"

"Ahhhhhh!" my brother and I screamed and ran back toward the house.

"It's just me!" yelled my dad. He had finished fixing the car and decided to scare us.

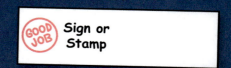

Discussion Challenge

1. Share about a time when you needed to fix something.
2. Explain why maps are important.
3. Should everyone have a flashlight in their house? why?

I needed to fix something <u>last week</u>. I was _____ when my _____ broke. In order to fix it, I _____.

- I agree with you about _____ because _____.

- I disagree with you about _____ because _____.

Maps are important for three reasons. First... Second... Third... This is why maps are important.

- I don't understand _____.
- Can you tell me more about _____.

Everyone should have a flashlight in their home for three reasons. First... Second... Finally... These are the reasons why...

- You're saying _____. Is that right?
- I like what you said about _____. I also think _____.

Rules:
- Speak 1 at a time.
- Respond to what others say by asking questions or making comments.

Sign or Stamp

Unit 7

Word Bank

1. 	2. 	3. 	4. 
5. 	6. Don't need more	7. 	8. 
9. Think something is true	10. 	11. 	12. 

enough
monster
believe
road

bush
scar
whisper
scream

mustache
kneel
bark
cave

 Sign or Stamp

Play "Who did it?" with a partner. Someone in the scene found your lost backpack and returned it to your house. You want to say thank you, but you have to find them first! One partner secretly chooses a person. The other asks yes/no questions to figure out who it is.

Was he/she

Example Questions

1. Was it a boy or a girl?
2. Was he wearing a fake mustache?   Yes, he was.   No, he wasn't.
3. Was he walking on the road?   Yes, she was.   No she wasn't.
4. Was he hiding behind some bushes?   Yes, he was.   No, he wasn't.
5. Was he carrying anything?   Yes, she was.   No, she wasn't.
6. Was he talking to anyone?   Yes, he was.   No, he wasn't.

Interview your classmates.

What were you doing yesterday at _____?

	Name:	Answer:
8:00 in the morning		
11:00 in the morning		
1:00 in the afternoon		
7:00 in the evening		
11:00 at night		

What was _____ doing yesterday at 8:00 in the evening?

	Name:	Answer:
your dad		
your mom		
your friend		
the T-Rex		
the cat		

The Criminal

Sally was walking her dog Spot one day when she saw a man with a mustache and a scar on his face hiding behind some bushes next to a cave. The man was looking at something.

Sally turned and saw a police car in the distance. Spot barked. The police car stopped.

The man scowled at Sally and then ran into the cave quickly. Spot and Sally hid behind a bush. "What is he doing?" Sally whispered. The police car came down the road towards the cave.

Suddenly, the man ran out of the cave screaming. A bear was chasing him. The police caught the man and put him in the car.

"I believe he is a criminal," said Sally, as she was starting to walk home again, "and I believe that might be a police bear."

"Ruff!" said Spot.

"Alright, alright," said Sally. "And I believe you are a police dog," she laughed. Spot barked happily.

Record Audio or Read to the Teacher

Sign or Stamp

Discussion Challenge

1. Do you believe in ghosts? Why or why not?
2. If you see a monster, what should you do?
3. Explain what a cave is. What kinds of animals live in caves?

I do/don't believe in ghosts for three reasons. First... Second... Finally... These are the reasons why...

- I agree with you about _____ because _____.

- I disagree with you about _____ because _____.

The best thing to do if you see a monster is to _____ because _____. Otherwise, if you don't, _____.

- I don't understand _____.
- Can you tell me more about _____.

A cave is _____. Many different kinds of animals call caves home. For example, _____.

- You're saying _____. Is that right?
- I like what you said about _____. I also think _____.

Rules:
- Speak 1 at a time.
- Respond to what others say by asking questions or making comments.

 Sign or Stamp

Unit 8

Word Bank

1. Month 1
2. Month 11
3. Month 2
4. Month 6
5. Month 5
6. Month 9
7. Month 4
8. Month 10
9. Month 12
10. Month 3
11. Month 8
12. Month 7

January
February
March
April

May
June
July
August

September
October
November
December

Sign or Stamp

Subject and Object Pronouns

Subject Pronouns	Verb	Object Pronouns
I		me
He		him
She	punched	her
It	kissed	it
You	jumped over	you
We	tickled	us
They		them

Find the subject pronouns.

1. He eats some ice cream every August.

2. They jumped on the bed in January.

3. We are going to go on vacation in September.

Find the object pronouns.

4. She kissed him in May.

5. My dad tickles me every March.

6. The teacher gave us a lot of homework in June.

Scripted Sentence Starters

1.

2.

3.

4.

5.

6.

Record Audio or Speak With the Teacher

 4 = bronze
5 = silver
6 = gold

1. A man walked by her house. She peeked out the window at him.

2. They had a meeting. The boss explained everything to them.

3. It was my birthday. My friend gave me a present.

4. My friend called me. I talked to her on the phone for an hour.

5. Class was over, and the teacher told us to line up.

6. (Make up your own sentence and draw.)

Just Be You, Sarah

Every month, Sarah likes to do something new. In January, she paints all her walls blue. In February, she wears her shoes on her head. In March, she sleeps underneath her bed. In April, she kisses every person she sees, and in May she decides to swing through some trees. In June and July, she skips and then drives. In August, she walks around giving high fives. September is special so she decides to wrestle until October arrives when she decides to eat pretzels. In November, she is getting tired of new things, but still she tries to sing everything. By December, she can't think of anything new, and her parents say, "You should just try being you."

Record Audio or Read to the Teacher

Sign or Stamp

Discussion Challenge

1. What is the best month of the year? Why?
2. If you could get rid of one month of the year, what month would you get rid of?
3. Compare and contrast October and April.

The best month of the year is _____ for three reasons. First... Second... Finally... These are the reasons why...

- I agree with you about _____ because _____.

- I disagree with you about _____ because _____.

If I could get rid of one month, I would get rid of _____. This would mean that _____.

- I don't understand _____.
- Can you tell me more about _____.

October and April are both similar and different. They are similar in that they _____. They are different _____.

- You're saying _____. Is that right?
- I like what you said about _____. I also think _____.

 Sign or Stamp

Unit 9

Word Bank

1. 	2. 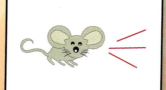	3. 	4. 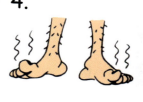
5. 	6. 	7. wait	8. Yum! 
9. 	10. 	11. 	12. 

log hold on stinky
squeak mouse woman
chop down mice women
delicious hole chase

Possessives

Possessive Adjectives	Possessive 's	Nouns
my	Mom's	pencil
his	my friend's	desk
her	the camel's	hair
its	the school's	stinky toes
your	the student's	lion
our	my grandpa's	spaceship
their	my teacher's	ugly dog

Find the possessive adjectives.

1. His spaceship is orange.
2. The mice ate her sandwich.
3. The dogs chased our car.

Find the words with possessive 's.

4. My dad's stinky toes stink really bad.
5. He jumped on the camel's back and rode away.
6. We flew to space in our teacher's spaceship.

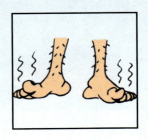

Make sentences using possessives.

1. Draw yourself.
2.
3.

4.
5. Draw you and your family.

Sentence Starters

1. That is my _____.
2. His _____ is _____.
3. Someone stole her _____.
4. They sold their _____.
5. Our _____ broke yesterday.

Record Audio or Speak With the Teacher

 5 = bronze
8 = silver
12 = gold

 Sign or Stamp

MR. SQUIRREL'S NEW HOME

Here is Mr. Squirrel. Isn't he cute? Here is his cute home in a cute tree...

Ah! Someone just chopped his tree down! Run Mr. Squirrel!

"But what about my home?" Mr. Squirrel asks.

We'll think of something. Just get out of there! Hey, look! There is a log over there. Why don't you try living in there?

"OK," says Mr. Squirrel.

"Hey! This is our home!" squeak a group of mice. "Go find somewhere else to live!"

"I'm so sorry! Someone cut down my tree and now I have nowhere to live."

"Why don't you try that hole over there," say the mice.

"Oh, great. Thanks!" says Mr. Squirrel.

"Hey!" says a snake. "This is not your home, and...hold on...you look delicious!"

Run faster Mr. Squirrel! The snake is chasing you!

"I know, but I don't know where else to go."

How about that tree over there with another cute little squirrel.

"Oh, OK," says Mr. Squirrel, running over to the tree.

"Hi there," says Mr. Squirrel to the other squirrel. "Someone chopped down my home and I was wondering if I could live here too."

"Sure. Come on in!"

Finally, Mr. Squirrel has a new cute home in a cute...

Ah! Someone just chopped the tree down!"

Record Audio or Read to the Teacher

Sign or Stamp

Discussion Challenge

1. Recount a time when you had mice in your house.
2. Explain what a log is.
3. Discuss why it is harmful to chop down too many trees in the world.

One time, we had mice in our house. We first noticed that _____. We decided to _____. Finally, _____.

A log is created in a few different ways. First, when someone chops... Also, when a tree gets old...

Chopping down too many trees is harmful for a few reasons. First... Furthermore... Finally... This is why we should protect our trees instead...

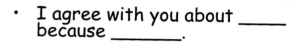

- I agree with you about _____ because _____.
- I disagree with you about _____ because _____.

- I don't understand _____.
- Can you tell me more about _____.

- You're saying _____. Is that right?
- I like what you said about _____. I also think _____.

Rules:
- Speak 1 at a time.
- Respond to what others say by asking questions or making comments.

 Sign or Stamp

Unit 10

Word Bank

1.
2.
3.
4.
5.

6. past/p.p. of **eat**
7.
8.
9. past/p.p. of **forget**
10. past/p.p. of **get**

11. past/p.p. of **fall**
12. past/p.p. of **hide**
13. past/p.p. of **take**
14. past/p.p. of **give**

borrow
lend
invite
sleeping bag
tent

take/took/taken
forget/forgot/forgotten
eat/ate/eaten
pack
call

give/gave/given
hide/hid/hidden
get/got/gotten
fall/fell/fallen

 Sign or Stamp

Present Perfect Tense

Rules students should know about the present perfect tense.

	+	?	-	
Present Perfect	have/has + P.P.	Have/Has	haven't/hasn't	before

P.P. = Past Participle (usually verb + ed, but often irregular)

Structure of a Present Perfect Tense Sentence

	Noun	Verb	Everything Else	When
1.	I	have jumped	on the bed	before
2.	You	have played	at school	before
3.	They	have followed	their mommy	before
4.	The teacher	has bought	pencils	before
5.	He	has eaten	a hamburger	before
6.	She	has gone	to her friend's house	before

Read the sentences below and talk about how they are different.

I played baseball yesterday.	He rode a bicycle last week.	They ate breakfast this morning.

I have played baseball before.	He has ridden a bicycle before.	They have eaten breakfast before.

Scripted Sentence Starters

Verb	Past Tense	Past Participle
borrow	borrowed	borrowed
buy	bought	bought
eat	ate	eaten
fall	fell	fallen
give	gave	given
hide	hid	hidden
take	took	taken
forget	forgot	forgotten
get	got	gotten

1. I

2. Tommy

3. I

4. The woman

5. The boy

6. The man

7. They

8. John

You can change underlined words (or any other words).
1. I have <u>painted</u> before.
2. Tommy has <u>borrowed a book</u> before.
3. I have <u>eaten</u> chips before.
4. The woman has <u>gone camping</u> before.
5. The boy has <u>hidden in the trash can</u> before.
6. The boss has <u>forgotten his belt</u> before.
7. They have <u>taken out the trash</u> before.
8. John has <u>gotten an F</u> before.

Record Audio or Speak With the Teacher

 4 = bronze
6 = silver
8 = gold

 Sign or Stamp

A CAMPING TRIP

Kelly is going camping with her family. She is pretty nervous because she has never gone camping before. Her dad has packed the car with all of their camping stuff. They have tents, sleeping bags, and food enough for three days in the woods.

"Don't be nervous, Kelly," says her dad. "This is going to be fun. You'll see!"

"What if a bear eats me?" Kelly asks.

"There aren't any bears, Kelly," her dad says.

"What if a crazy man with a mustache and a scar on his face steals all of our food and we die from hunger?" asks Kelly.

"Very interesting. I think you have watched too many movies. I don't think there are any bad guys with mustaches and scars running around in the woods," says her dad.

"What if a terrible monster comes to sleep in our tent when we are sleeping and we wake up in the morning and scream and the monster gets scared and eats us?" asks Kelly.

"There aren't any monsters either," says her dad.

Then Kelly's mom asks, "What if there's a dinosaur living in a cave and…"

"OK! OK!" cries Kelly's dad. "Take everything out of the car!"

"Why?" asks Kelly and her mom.

"We're going to camp in the living room instead."

Record Audio or Read to the Teacher

Discussion Challenge

1. What are the most important things you need when you go camping?
2. Explain the difference between "borrow" and "lend."
3. If you could only invite one person to your birthday party, who would you invite and why?

If you are going camping, there are many important things you need to bring. First... Also... Then... Finally...

 • I agree with you about ____ because _____.

 • I disagree with you about ____ because _____.

The words borrow and lend are similar but different. When you borrow something... By contrast, when you lend something...

 • I don't understand _____.
• Can you tell me more about _____.

If I could only invite one person to my birthday party, I would invite ____. There are three reasons for this. The first reason is.... Secondly... Lastly...

 • You're saying _____. Is that right?
• I like what you said about ____. I also think _____.

Rules:
- Speak 1 at a time.
- Respond to what others say by asking questions or making comments.

 Sign or Stamp

Unit 11

Word Bank

1. past/p.p. of **see**	2. past/p.p. of **go**	3. past/p.p. of **choose**	4. past/p.p. of **be**
5. past/p.p. of **do**	6. past/p.p. of **break**	7. past/p.p. of **steal**	8. past/p.p. of **speak**
9. past/p.p. of **wear**	10. past/p.p. of **ride**	11. past/p.p. of **write**	12. past/p.p. of **drive**

do/did/done   break/broke/broken   ride/rode/ridden
see/saw/seen   steal/stole/stolen   write/wrote/written
be/was,were/been   speak/spoke/spoken   drive/drove/driven
go/went/gone   wear/wore/worn
  choose/chose/chosen

Sign or Stamp

Scripted Sentence Starters

Verb	Past Tense	Past Participle
do	did	done
see	saw	seen
be	was/were	been
go	went	gone
break	broke	broken
steal	stole	stolen
speak	spoke	spoken
wear	wore	worn
choose	chose	chosen
ride	rode	ridden
write	wrote	written
drive	drove	driven

1. I
2. Tammy
3. The thief
4. He
5. The cow ✗
6. The students ✗
7. They ✗
8. He ✗

You can change underlined words (or any other words).

1. Have you <u>driven a car</u> yet? Yes, I have.
2. Has Tammy <u>spoken English</u> yet? Yes, she has.
3. Has the thief <u>stolen the TV</u> yet? Yes, he has.
4. Has he <u>written a story</u> yet? Yes, he has.
5. Has the cow <u>worn a dress</u> yet? No, it hasn't.
6. Have the students <u>chosen books</u> yet? No, they haven't.
7. Have they <u>seen an elephant</u> yet? No, they haven't.
8. Has he <u>ridden a camel</u> yet? No, he hasn't.

Record Audio or Speak With the Teacher

 4 = bronze
6 = silver
8 = gold

 Sign or Stamp

The Criminal

Bam went the car door...I mean the security fence.

"What was that?" cried Larry. He looked out the window of his tree house. There, on the other side of the yard, was the most dangerous, dastardly, evil, really bad criminal in the whole world.

"Fuzzy," Larry said to his stuffed teddy bear, "There's a dangerous, dastardly, evil, really bad criminal trying to break through our defenses! He has broken through the fence and jumped over the river already!"

"Don't worry!" said Fuzzy. "Bubbles will stop him."

"Nope. He has just gotten past Bubbles, too."

"Has he found the secret hole yet?"

"Yep, he has just come through the hole to the other side, taken our pizza and stolen...our treasure. This means war!"

"Let's go show that dastardly criminal that no one takes our pizza...or treasure!" said Fuzzy.

"Attack!" Larry and Fuzzy yelled as they climbed out of the tree house and ran across the yard.

Then, Larry's dad said, "Larry, go wash your hands for dinner. And, if you attack me again, you'll go to bed without any pizza or ice cream."

"Oh, hmm, I see" said Larry, stopping. He looked down at Fuzzy, then back at his dad. "Well played, Dad. Well played."

His dad groaned and walked into the house.

"I'll just go wash my hands then," said Larry.

What's happening?

The bad guy has broken the fence already.

The Criminal

Can you make sentences about what the criminal has done?

Discussion Challenge

1. What languages do you speak? How are they different from English?
2. Have you ever broken anything before? Recount the experience.
3. Have you ever ridden a horse, camel, elephant or other animal? Recount the experience.

I speak _____. _____ is different from English in a few ways. One... Second... Third...

I have broken _____ before. I was _____ one day when _____. Afterward, I _____. From the experience, I learned _____.

I have ridden _____ before. It was a _____ experience. First... Then.... Afterward... I would/wouldn't do it again.

- I agree with you about ____ because _____.
- I disagree with you about ____ because _____.

- I don't understand _____.
- Can you tell me more about _____.

- You're saying _____. Is that right?
- I like what you said about ____. I also think _____.

Rules:
- Speak 1 at a time.
- Respond to what others say by asking questions or making comments.

Sign or Stamp

Unit 12

Word Bank

1.
2.
3. When someone gets something you don't
4. Something you have to do
5. past/p.p. of **say**
6. past/p.p. of **sell**
7. past/p.p. of **sit**
8. past/p.p. of **write**
9. past/p.p. of **ride**
10. past/p.p. of **forget**
11. past/p.p. of **find**
12. past/p.p. of **fall**

make your bed
rule
it's not fair
wash the dishes

say/said/said
write/wrote/written
find/found/found
ride/rode/ridden
forget/forgot/forgotten

fall/fell/fallen
have,has/had/had
sit/sat/sat
sell/sold//sold

 Sign or Stamp

for	**since**
for five years	since I was eight years old
for six months	since 2008
for three days	since last year
for a long time	since I was young

1. How long have you played _____?

the piano

the guitar

the violin

the recorder

the drums

video games

2. How long have you had _____?

I have played the piano for three years.
I have played video games since last year.
I have had a fish for two weeks.
I have had a bicycle since I was eight.

Record Audio or Speak With the Teacher

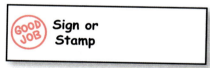

Negatives with For or Since

When it has been a long time since you have done something, you can use the negative present perfect with for or since

1. When was the last time you saw _____?

2. When was the last time you _____? (Use a Past Tense Verb)

I haven't seen my grandparents for two weeks
I haven't seen a dentist for five months.
I haven't ridden a horse for two years.
I haven't written a story since last week.

Record Audio or Speak With the Teacher

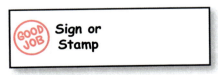

Responsibilities

"Go wash the dishes, please," said Jacky's mom, one morning after breakfast.

"Why do I always have to wash the dishes?" complained Jacky.

"You haven't washed the dishes for three months!" yelled her mom.

"Oh," said Jacky.

"When you're done, go make your bed," said her mom.

"It's not fair! Why do I always have to make my bed?" complained Jacky.

"Because you slept in it! That's the rule!" yelled her mom.

"Oh," said Jacky. "I forgot."

"Don't forget to feed the dog!" said her mom.

"We have a dog?" asked Jacky.

"Oh, my word!" yelled her mom. "We have had a dog for ten years!"

"Right. I know that. I was just testing you, Mom."

"I have a test for you too," said Jacky's mom. "How long have you lived in this house?"

"Um, since I was born?" Jacky said.

"That's right, and if you'd like to keep living in it, you had better start taking better responsibility for your jobs."

Discussion Challenge

1. What rules do you have at your house? Do you think they are good rules? What would you change?
2. Recount an experience when you thought something was unfair.
3. If you were president of the world, what rules would you create to make the world a better place?

At my house, we have ____ rules. First... Second... Third. I would change ____ because ____.

 • I agree with you about ____ because ____.

 • I disagree with you about ____ because ____.

One experience I thought was unfair happened <u>last week</u>. I was ____. Then... It was unfair because ____.

 • I don't understand ____.
• Can you tell me more about ____.

If I were president of the world, I would create ____ rules. First... Second... Third... These rules would make the world a better place because...

 • You're saying ____. Is that right?
• I like what you said about ____. I also think ____.

Sign or Stamp

Unit 13

Word Bank

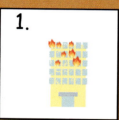
1.

2. scared but still do it (adj)

3. scared but still do it (noun)

4.

5.

6.

7. What is Happening Around the World

8.

9.

10.

11.

12.

13.

14.

15.

news
building
burn
brave
courage

grab
escape
factory
save
rescue

pollute
hospital
bleed
protest
river

Sign or Stamp

Do lots of activities with this page to practice making past and present perfect tense sentences with these irregular verbs.

	Past Tense	Past Participle (P.P)
break	broke	broken
choose	chose	chosen
eat	ate	eaten
fall	fell	fallen
give	gave	given
grow	grew	grown
hide	hid	hidden
ride	rode	ridden
steal	stole	stolen
take	took	taken
throw	threw	thrown
write	wrote	written
speak	spoke	spoken
fly	flew	flown
drive	drove	driven
forget	forgot	forgotten
see	saw	seen
blow	blew	blown
draw	drew	drawn
get	got	gotten
wear	wore	worn
find	found	found
be	was/were	been
make	made	made
sweep	swept	swept
fight	fought	fought
buy	bought	bought
say	said	said
leave	left	left
have	had	had
sleep	slept	slept
sell	sold	sold
hear	heard	heard
catch	caught	caught
read	read	read
run	ran	run
tell	told	told

Factory Protest

"This is ACB news and we have a special report from our reporter Jack Jackson. We go to him live now. Jack."

"Hi, this is Jack Jackson. With ACB news. People are protesting the factory that you see behind me. The old factory has polluted the river in this neighborhood for years and the people are angry. As you can see... Ahhhh!

"The factory just caught on fire! Whoa!

"There are people trying to escape the burning building! Watch out! The firefighters have arrived. They are bravely running in to the building to save people. Be careful!

"One man is bleeding and somebody has grabbed a shirt to put on his wound!

"Now, the ambulance is taking people to a nearby hospital.

"This has been very scary. Jack Jackson, ACB news, back to you in the news room."

Don't write. Just say the answers.

Practice together as a class a few times and then try to do it individually.

1. The alien _____ a hot dog before. (eat)

2. We _____ our bicycles yesterday at two o'clock. (ride)

3. Tom _____ to school every day. (go)

4. They _____ some broccoli yesterday. (throw)

5. I _____ my homework right now. (do)

6. She _____ her grandma last week. (see)

7. I _____ to Japan before. (be)

Sign or Stamp

Discussion Challenge

1. Recount an experience when you or someone you know needed to be brave.
2. Explain how to escape a burning building.
3. What is fake news and why is it harmful?

One time when ____ needed to be brave was <u>last year</u>. ____ was _____, when_____. Then... Afterward...

In order to escape a burning building, you need to do three things. First... Second... Third... A burning building is very dangerous, so...

Fake news is news that is _____. The reason that it is harmful is because _____. If we can't tell what is real, then _____. This is why...

- I agree with you about _____ because _____.

- I disagree with you about ____ because _____.

- I don't understand _____.
- Can you tell me more about _____.

- You're saying _____. Is that right?
- I like what you said about ____. I also think _____.

Sign or Stamp

Unit 14

Word Bank

1. Make something new
2.
3.
4.  rug
5.
6.
7.
8.
9.
10.
11.
12.

invent
sweep
turn on
electricity

wash the laundry
change the sheets
mow the lawn
vacuum cleaner

oil
boss
broom
carpet

 Sign or Stamp

63

Scripted Sentence Starters

	+	**?**	**-**	🕐
Present Tense:	verb (He/She/It → S)	Do/Does	(don't/doesn't)	every day
Present Cont:	be verb + verb + ing	Be-Verb	(am not/isn't/aren't)	right now
Future Tense:	be verb + going to + verb	Be-Verb	(am not/isn't/aren't)	tomorrow
Past Tense:	verb + ed (ate, hid, fell)	Did	didn't	yesterday
Past Cont:	be verb + verb + ing	Was/Were	(wasn't/weren't)	yesterday at 2
Present Perfect:	have/has + P.P.	Have/Has	(haven't/hasn't)	before/already/ yet for/since

1. What time  at 6:00 every day

2. What  right now

3. When  next summer

4. When  last weekend

5. What  when the aliens came

6. How long  2 years

1. What time does he <u>get up</u> every day?
   He <u>gets up</u> at 6:00 every day.
2. What is she doing right now?
   She is <u>sweeping</u> right now.
3. When are you going to <u>go on vacation</u>?
   I am going to <u>go on vacation</u> next summer.
4. When did he <u>throw eggs on his eyes</u>?
   He <u>threw eggs on his eyes</u> last weekend.
5. What was she doing when the aliens came?
   She was <u>washing the dishes</u> when the aliens came.
6. How long have they <u>studied English</u>?
   They have <u>studied English</u> for 2 years.

Record Audio or Speak With the Teacher

4 = bronze
5 = silver
6 = gold

 Sign or Stamp

Don't write. Just say the answers.

Practice together as a class a few times and then try to do it individually.

1. My mom _____ the car last night. (drive)

2. The lion _____ the rabbit right now. (approach)

3. Sally _____ the floor yesterday at 8:00. (sweep)

4. I _____ a camel before. (ride)

5. The gorilla _____ its homework every day. (do)

6. My friend _____ a movie every weekend. (watch)

7. I _____ to Disneyland next week. (travel)

Sign or Stamp

DR. CRAZY, THE CRAZY MAD SCIENTIST

Dr. Crazy was a mad scientist. He wanted to invent something amazing.

"How about an airplane?!" said Dr. Crazy. "I want to travel around the world."

"They have been invented already," said his assistant.

"Ah, man!" said Dr. Crazy. "Ooh, how about a vacuum cleaner! I hate sweeping with a broom. I could sweep the carpet so fast with a vacuum cleaner."

"They have already been invented," said his assistant.

"Ah, man!" said Dr. Crazy. "I got it! I will invent a switch to turn on a light. When you hit the switch, the electricity will travel to the light and the light will light up! That would be amazing!"

"They have already been invented," said his assistant. "You used a light switch to turn on the light in this room when you came in. I am going to quit this job. You're crazy, Dr. Crazy."

"You can't quit!" said Dr. Crazy.

"I'm your boss! Hey! What about oil?! I could invent oil to cook food with so that food wouldn't stick to the pan!"

"I'm leaving now. Bye!"

"How about a vacuum cleaner!"

"You already said that!"

Discussion Challenge

1. What are some of the different ways you use electricity every day?
2. What chores do you have around your house? Do you think it is fair that you have chores?
3. If you could invent a machine to help you with your chores, what would you invent?

I use electricity in a number of ways every day. First… Also… Lastly… Electricity is an important part of my life.

- I agree with you about _____ because _____.

- I disagree with you about _____ because _____.

I have _____ chores at my house. My first chore is… My second…. Finally, my third chore.. I think it is fair/unfair because…

- I don't understand _____.
- Can you tell me more about _____.

If I could invent one machine to help me with my chores, it would be _____. With a _____, I could… I would also be able to….

- You're saying _____. Is that right?
- I like what you said about _____. I also think _____.

Sign or Stamp

Unit 15

Word Bank

1.
2.
3.
4.
5.
6.
7. Something People Do Passed Down from Their Parents and Grandparents
8.
9.
10.
11.

kindness
decorate
culture
chimney

tradition
reindeer
candle
fireworks

present
gift
celebrate

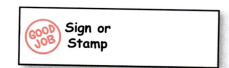

Sign or Stamp

Scripted Sentence Starters

	+	**?**	**−**	
Present Tense:	verb (He/She/It -> S)	Do/Does	(don't/doesn't)	every day
Present Cont:	be verb + verb + ing	Be-Verb	(am not/isn't/aren't)	right now
Future Tense:	be verb + going to + verb	Be-Verb	(am not/isn't/aren't)	tomorrow
Past Tense:	verb + ed (ate, hid, fell)	Did	didn't	yesterday
Past Cont:	be verb + verb + ing	Was/Were	(wasn't/weren't)	yesterday at 2
Present Perfect:	have/has + P.P.	Have/Has	(haven't/hasn't)	before/already/yet for/since

1. When/he

every year

2. What/they

right now

3. When/the reindeer

on Christmas Eve

4. When/Santa

last weekend

5. What/she

yesterday afternoon at 2:00

6. How long/you/celebrate

Diwali
Hanukkah
Chinese New Year
Christmas
Kwanzaa
Other Holiday

1. When does he get presents?
He gets presents every year at Christmas.
2. What are they doing right now?
They are decorating the Christmas tree right now.
3. When are the reindeer gong to come?
They are going to come on Christmas eve.

Record Audio or Speak With the Teacher

 4 = bronze
6 = silver
8 = gold

 Sign or Stamp

Don't write. Just say the answers.

Practice together as a class a few times and then try to do it individually.

1. My mom ✗ _____ the car last night. (drive)

2. The lion ✗ _____ the rabbit right now. (approach)

3. Sally ✗ _____ the floor yesterday at 8:00. (sweep)

4. I ✗ _____ a camel before. (ride)

5. The gorilla ✗ _____ its homework every day. (do)

6. My friend ✗ _____ a movie every weekend. (watch)

7. I ✗ _____ to America next week. (travel)

Sign or Stamp

Holidays Around the World

In the United States, Christmas is a major holiday that many people celebrate. The U.S. version of Christmas has been spread around the world through popular movies and businesses. Decorating a Christmas tree is a common tradition, and everyone knows the story of Santa Claus flying around the world with his eight reindeer, sliding down chimneys to give presents to well-behaved children everywhere.

As you probably know though, many people around the world, and in the United States, celebrate Christmas differently or don't celebrate Christmas at all.

Chinese people, for instance, celebrate Chinese New Year. In late January or early February, kids are out of school and parents are off work. There are big family gatherings where everyone eats lots of delicious traditional foods, people let off firecrackers, and adults give children red envelopes with money inside.

Jewish people celebrate Hanukkah, also known as the Festival of Lights. Each year, Jewish people gather with their families to light candles on a Menorah, eat traditional foods, play games, and say prayers together.

Many people from African cultures celebrate Kwanzaa which is a six-day celebration that ends with a big feast. People light candles on a Kinara, perform traditional music and discuss African history.

Another big holiday around the time of Christmas is Diwali, also called the Festival of Lights, that comes from Indian culture. On this holiday, the Indian people celebrate the life and victory of good over evil with their families, lighting off fireworks, and eating big meals.

The world is full of many different, beautiful cultures that celebrate different holidays. Most of them though involve family, food and fun. What holidays do you celebrate?

Discussion Challenge

1. What holidays do you celebrate? What traditions do you have during that holiday?
2. How is kindness important when people have different cultures?
3. Compare and contrast two holidays that you find interesting.

I celebrate _____. During _____, we _____, _____, and _____. It is a wonderful holiday.

Kindness is important when people have different cultures for three reasons. First... Second... Third... These are their reasons kindness...

Two holidays I find interesting are _____ and _____. They are similar in that they both _____. They are also different. _____ whereas _____.

- I agree with you about _____ because _____.

- I disagree with you about _____ because _____.

- I don't understand _____.
- Can you tell me more about _____.

- You're saying _____. Is that right?
- I like what you said about _____. I also think _____.

 Sign or Stamp

Copyright 2023

Kid-Inspired Classroom

All rights reserved. No part of this book may be reproduced in any form.

Made in the USA
Middletown, DE
30 August 2024

59847967R00042